WHAT MINIMAL JOY

About Michael Favala Goldman's writing

Michael Favala Goldman is a stealth poet. The plain language and deep meaning of his poems can reverberate to the core of your being.

—Lynette Yetter, Poetry Translation finalist 2023 PEN Awards

Goldman's poems are succinct and subtle, understated even, yet powerful and persuasive; one after another, they take the reader by quiet surprise.

—Barry DeCarli, author of *Camouflage of Noise* and *Silence*

These are the poems we need in this human moment, at the sticky end of the pandemic. Goldman's transcendent vulnerability underscores how little we have, and how precious and resilient it is, after all.

—Sara Eddy, author of the poetry collection *Full Mouth*

What sparkles in Goldman's work is that the voice is both sweet and edgy. There is a slight tone of annoyance, a touch of anger, that compliments the quiet sweetness. The clash, the juxtaposition of these forces gives way to a voice that is proper. By 'proper' I mean real, a series of tropes that captures the nuances of the human experience, of the human tumble down the stairs of everyday life.

—Matthem Lippmann,
author of *Mesmerizingly Sadly Beautiful*,
winner of the Levis Prize in Poetry

These poems recognize the spiritual implications of quotidian moments and objects in daily life. They gently expose, with warm humor and piercing honesty, the unbridgeable separateness of each person, while also holding up for the reader examples of the sometimes difficult yet unbreakable connections between each of us.

—Mark Luebbers,
author of the poetry collection *Flat Light*,
co-author of *Citizens of Ordinary Time*
and the chapbook *Group Portrait*

Filled with grace and with rage, with confessions of dreams and proclamations of lies, remnants, victories and failures, a light so finely weaved into poems by a writer who also understands darkness. What minimal joy, what sharp mixture of feelings, something for everyone... most of all, a reminder: We are the only cure for the trouble we cause.

    —Elizabeth Torres,
    Colombian-American poet multimedia artist
    and literary translator. Author of *Lotería*,
    winner of the 2022 Ambroggio prize

Pithy, poignant, thoughtful meditations on what matters most: love, aging, loss, and connection. Goldman's poems will help you see life, romance, and friendship in a more incandescent light.

    —Lanette Sweeney,
    author of *What I Should Have Said: A Poetry Memoir*
    about Losing a Child to Addiction

Goldman's poems leave us in a rich wake of stories, meanings, and contradictions inherent in being human. He transforms daily moments in fresh and playful ways, building poems everywhere, suggesting why a soul might stick around.

    —Sharon Tracey, author of *Land Marks*

Grounded and ethereal. Goldman's poems run the gamut: the pain, the pleasure, the awe, and the confusion of being. Deceptive meditations on everyday living reveal the greater truths of existence. A brilliant reminder of the magnitude experience.

    —A.M. Larks, *Kelp Journal*

What Minimal Joy

Michael Favala Goldman

SPUYTEN DUYVIL
New York City

ACKNOWLEDGMENTS:

If Vladimir Putin could die from periodontitis;
Working at the UN International Crime Tribunal; Remnant;
In case you were wondering
Wordpeace, summer, 2022

Hologram of the Infinite
30 Poems in November, 2021

Solidarity
Northampton Biennial, 2022

Testimony; In the realm of forms
Meat for Tea, summer, 2022

Punctuation; Puppy; About seven pm.
The Writing is on the Walls, 2023

Jellyfish/You are
Kelp Journal, 2023

With appreciation to my editors Libby and LInda and to all the
people, named and unnamed, who appear in these poems. You
help me to recognize the poetry in life.

CONTENTS

Acknowledgments

III.

WHAT MINIMAL JOY

1

WORD OF THE YEAR

I named my new puppy Pandemic.
He's growing all the time.

We go for a lot of walks.
He gets into everything.

I try and do what you're supposed to
so I have to say no a lot.

Sometimes it feels like
he's training me.

I think we are bonding.
He follows me around.

I get nervous when we are near others,
afraid he'll jump.

The longer we're together I forget
what my life was like before.

TURNING POINT

Recently I encountered
my starving artist
observing my relentless activity
these past fifteen years
these past fifteen minutes
with his sunken eyes.

He is patient as ice.
I have been taught
not to encourage him
that once you give him
a handout he won't
leave you alone.

WHAT DID YOU DO THIS MORNING?

I had just been sharing some poetry
via email with a generous friend
and I had had leftover crepes for breakfast
with sunflower butter, chocolate, and
black currant jam and the electrician
had just left after running a cable
to our soon-to-be porch fan
twelve years in the making
and I had slept soundly last night
my wife beside me after she
had been away and I'm not sure
what happened exactly,
but it felt like love
was about to overtake my body
and God was going to start
speaking, but
nothing happened. I lay down
and it passed, or at least mostly.

OUT OF NOWHERE

Faced with my mind
I'm defenseless

I'm barely awake
and already it's upon me

seems to know
my weaknesses

has no qualms
about taking over.

IN THE REALM OF FORMS

after Plato

An ideal bed.
An ideal mosquito.
An ideal tree.
Anyone can recognize them.

In my mind
an ideal you
hounding my reality
like an adamant specter.

Meanwhile
I take myself for granted
can't see how
I can be improved.

Project your shadows
onto my cave walls
so I can find
my way out.

You as a Giraffe

Cautiously approach the water
nervously glance around
legs slowly splaying
neck lowering bit by bit.

A moment later you are loping
across the savannah's supple grass,
sunlight a warm blessing, as if
survival were always easy.

ESSENCE

Sometimes a woman is a spiral
a shell like a whelk worn away
by salt water in waves
tumbled to a core
of smooth edges, pink lobes, alive
in still inner dance
like the turning of all things
rounded and complete.

Jellyfish/You are

mostly water
in an odd-shaped bag
with a few strings attached.

THIS BAG IS MADE OF 100% RECYCLED PLASTIC

a litterbag in a Danish train car

Using trash to hold trash
is as good an idea
as any

Maybe extending the lifespan
of plastic
somehow extends our own

Perhaps long enough
for us to save ourselves
from ourselves.

WHAT I'M UP AGAINST

Desire and logic
have not met.

Craving swells,
temporarily eclipses

whatever discipline
I thought I had.

The body, the heart
the soul—

who am I
to stand in my way?

Given the right
conditions

I could betray
everyone and everything

for a brief mistake
for a brief reward.

You sent me
this symbol
for breathe

which immediately
became my answer
to every problem

loss
hurt
shock

lungs know how
to buttress
the heart.

ENDEAVOR

Instead of excusing yourself
from life like a paper doll,
gain girth, curves, flesh,
for glee and grief to plunge
and poke. Grow intimate
with sensation and your body
will be everything.

WHY YOUR SOUL IS STICKING AROUND

To keep the conversation going

To see what happens

To find a way back.

BASIS

It is the things
we do not understand
which make life go.

The wind, the mind
The Earth turning tilted
just so.

2

A BIT OF A SCRAMBLE

Hiking Mt. Kearsarge on our anniversary

I count a thousand ways
to sprain an ankle
between the rocks, the roots,
the ice, the mud, and we
evade them all. The real danger
is in becoming absorbed
in my own steps, my own body
ambling ahead and losing
you. Remember we are doing this
together, one more summit,
past the frost line, to the wind,
the view of mountains.

WHEN MY SON TOLD ME

he was going to propose
marriage to his beloved

tears welled in my eyes
not from known feelings

more a pressure or echo
from generations past

now coming through
him, through me, the future

being created, squeezing
through my heart and throat

I could barely get out the words,
"I'm so happy for you."

I HAD NOT THOUGHT THIS THROUGH

We were lying
in bed.

I imagined you
with someone else

and my heart filled
with dread.

I could not
let that happen.

So I asked you
to marry me.

There was no
discussion.

You said yes
without hesitation

and that fear
went to sleep.

RITUAL

Upon waking
I take you
in my arms

You tell me
what is not
quite right

With you
or me
or others

It's embarrassing
the way you
expose us

It must be tiring
to be right
all the time.

THE OTHER ME

I am jealous of myself
for being yours
for being naked with you
for talking in private
for knowing things
for making you blush.

If I were in my place
I would savor more
each greeting
each inch of skin
think more of myself
be who you deserve.

Risk Benefit

Investing in you
in us
is no sure thing
no quick windfall scheme

More like a bond
with a foreign entity
which could go
either way

My surplus
has been dwindling
with expenses
plus devaluations

Your exchange
appears safe
has a reassuring
boilerplate

I am sitting tight
holding onto
this modest
position.

Murmuration

Poetry critique group, Nov. 14, 2021

They find
one another by
song or by instinct
arrive from their nests
shadows dark against
the sky flying in precise
formation wings near-
ly touching each an
integral part of the
complete wave
pattern where they
remain briefly
before returning
from solidarity
to their own
solitary
flight.

PUNCTUATION

Sometimes a comma
is a kiss between
two independent clauses,

sometimes an ellipsis
is several kisses
coming to a gentle pause...

sometimes a period
is a kiss
at the end.

PUPPY

The kind of love
that's all over you

your face, your mouth,
your eyes, your crevices.

Unselfconscious, soft, damp,
everywhere at once.

The kind instinctively
you push away.

Overwhelming
is not pleasing.

And anyway,
isn't impetuous love,

to put it bluntly,
a little much?

MORNING

You crawled on top of me,
sat on my waist,
caressed my arms, underarms,
my hairy chest, its bones,
my belly, its soft concavity,
and my mind could have bolted
like a horse pulling a chariot
down an ancient track,
but I kept breathing, softening
the animal of my body,
letting it receive touch,
though you leaned down
and kissed me I did not turn
ambitious and hard, my lips
stayed plump and limp.
When you peeled your legs,
your body, off of mine
to greet the day,
I had no regret.

INFATUATION

When I am with you
I can't imagine wanting
to be somewhere else

and then it's over

I imagine you
showing up places
you have never been

I see you
fit into spaces occupied
by people you don't know

and my heart is confused
by your absence
by your presence.

INCLINATION

My ego always
faces one way
keeping a lookout

The other side
is unexplored
touchy

Sometimes you
remind me of it
which I do not appreciate

Stay on my good side
and we will go
round and round.

GRAVITY

under certain conditions
under general observation

objects fall
at a constant rate

but
at a curious elevation

or
in a discrepancy of time

the heart falls
at its own
speed.

Between Christmas and New Year's

The Berkshires, 2021

Snow is coming down
heavier than air
the water cycle
doing its thing
in the quietest way.

Tracey calls me
on the phone
asks about breaking up
with her guy.
I ask if she thinks
she can save him
and herself
at the same time.
But will he drink
himself to death? she asks.
I say we all have wounds.
Sometimes being
with another person
makes them hurt more.
She says she knows
that about hurting.
She is just trying
to figure out
how to do this
with the least pain.

The snow keeps falling
covers everything
like a cold bandage.

LOVE IS NOT FOR SISSIES

You steep in my anger
before I even acknowledge it.

I must feel your pain
before you can forgive me.

You need to risk
chasing me away.

I have to admit
to throwing your love back at you.

We are the only cure
for the trouble we cause.

EVERY DAY WITH YOU

The stakes go higher
like on a game show.
Will I be a winner
or will I lose it all
on the next question.

CRAMPED VILLANELLE

There's an elephant in the room.
Let's use a Ouija board to learn its name.
Maybe we can shoo it with a broom.

Our sound barrier might break with a boom
when we tell the other they're to blame
for there being an elephant in the room.

You know what happens when you assume
and deny the reasons why it came.
Maybe we can shoo it with a broom.

Could it be an old ghost in a costume
who lost its way and wandered to our game
becoming an elephant in the room?

Haven't you smelled its unbearable perfume?
I'm afraid to check if it's tame.
Maybe we could shoo it with a broom.

Would the emptiness be too much to presume?
And who will clean the leftover shame?
Maybe we can shoo it with a broom.
There's an elephant in the room.

BITTERSWEET

Despite how you give
Despite how I give

Despite how you love
Despite how I love

You will never belong
I will never belong

You chose me
I chose you

Despite my shortcomings
Despite your shortcomings

I am all you have
You are all I have.

MR. AND MRS. B SIT AND STARE AT THEIR PLOT

They picked it out together,
the one near the bench.

They sit and cry
for many reasons.

Partners married
over forty years

often die
within two weeks
of each other.

Life so full and then
so narrow.

And ending
so soon.

About 7 pm.

You were putting leftovers
in plastic containers,
I was putting away
clean dishes
we ended up
beside each other
at the counter
without a thought
fully forming
our lips met
gently and
stayed.

I felt your knees bend
slightly changing
the angle
and my knees dipped
my lips
caught yours
your mouth
opened a little
taking in
my upper lip
my tongue tasted
your lip
felt its wet wrinkles
while our bellies
were meeting
as were our breasts
and our breath
each of us an arm
and a hand

on the small
of the other's back
we exhaled
our lips
parted
and with a sigh
each we returned
to cleaning up.

SIGNALS

At the micro level
particles are oscillating
in and out of existence

My body, my nerves
are only here
half the time

Like starlight
we come together
blinking.

WHAT WE DO

When evening is done
we settle in bed,
naked, embracing
arms, legs,
in the dark.

What happened before
is mostly shed
as we enter the night
bringing nothing with us
but the other.

September

The harvest moon is waning
and we are in our late fifties.

The moon will come around again
eventually, its orbit apparently
not winding down with time,
which is not winding down either.

Age is a product
of living with time.

Things oblivious of time,
squarely in the now,
keep cycling and cycling.

Eons pass without their noticing,
having no memory,
no expectation,
nothing to regret.

3

Something for Everyone

Aalborg, Denmark

Jomfru Ane Gade is a narrow street
with clubs and bars on both sides,
tables full outside the establishments
nightly with revelers, extroverts,
bleach-blondes, bikers, escape artists
and others obliterating loneliness.

In the morning the communal street
sweeper swishes through like a tiny
steamroller erasing the debris of memory
littering the asphalt. From the hotel
I can't hear the young women with
bare midriffs expounding on a recent
sms exchange or the men singing snippets
of a syrupy pop song. I can't hear laughter
or chairs scraping or the dwindling
slightly slurred shouts of goodbye.

My window faces the harbor without a boat
as the orange glare rises like a fiery stain
from the water, between the sharp concrete
edge of the promenade colossus and the factory
silhouettes, smoke-stacked rectangles,
clouds of fumes or steam rising in plumes
that unite and then unite again with the gray
clouds in the gray sky as if they were needed,
and always would be there to make clouds and
join the sky to the machinations of man.

Hologram of the infinite

You are built of bits
and leave bits

everywhere
just like me.

You pick up traces
without even trying

in your breath
on your skin

ash from volcanoes
photons from stars.

You are a repository
an encyclopedia

where the universe
can look up anything.

You don't need to be
self-aware

you just need
to look around.

Whatever you discover
was already here.

If all else
were obliterated

I could be recreated
from you.

ADAM

If I really am created
in God's image,
no wonder things
are dicey.

And if everyone else
is too,
that explains a lot.

More of the same

The variety astounding,
from remarkably similar
sets of DNA and cells,
we are those who produce
rocket ships, drug abuse,
word games, textile color schemes,
entomology, and extortion.
There is no predicament
or field of research
too sacred or profane
but people will be there,
while the planet and universe
spin in unconcerned space,
and despite our fear
and cognition,
individualism
and solidarity,
no one can say
where
this
leads.

GLOWWORM

What minimal joy! Star-descended
celestial on the damp night ground
exuding humble light. An invitation
to life? To death? Too dim to see by,
but visible. Not really wanting
anyone to know, yet unable
to keep it to yourself.

Emerald Glass Frog

Espadarana prosoblepon

Do not go hunting for them.
Life's jewels are better
left alone. Let them
come looking for you.

ADJUSTMENTS

she was going to become a dog trainer
not just any dog trainer
one who could take a snarling menace
and remind it of its puppy self
that actually
there is nothing
to be afraid of.

but after a series of administrative
positions and a long-term
relationship betrayal, which she thinks
she probably deserved
and she would never be
so blue-eyed again,
she ended up someplace
in the middle of life
like a piece in a board game.

she was working on cultivating
gratitude for life
as it was
while self-medicating
somewhat unconsciously
surviving and doing
intricate and gorgeous
counted cross-stitch.

she got a dog
which adored her
but she only walked it
once a day. In fact,
it was easier
to just let it
out into the yard.

SALT CREEK LANE

We were riding out to Lawson's place,
I was on the roof of the tractor
flicking down pebbles
lodged in a crease in the metal.

We passed the big oak with the gnarled roots
where the man's drill was going 'round
in the mud and I saw it, the mud getting darker
going from brown to black.

The man in his clean flannel shirt
and blue denims was telling us
what the future was going to be like,
how he would give, say, $60,000
to each of his neighbors—
he didn't even have to know them well—
because what was he going to do with it
after he had seven million and a boat,
and so did his wife.

He turned away and puffed
on his cigar. The smoke was the smell
of sadness, how money could displace
human connection from one day
to the next, and no way back.

THIS OLD MAN

He played once
and play became work
with knick-knacks

He worked once
and work became life
with knick-knacks

He lived once
and life became death
with knick-knacks.

SMILE

for Ghita Nørby

I am sorry about
your happy childhood

where your impossible shadows
hung by their arms

where the dinner table was severed
with strong lights, heavy food

where your deep need was stowed
below the floorboards

pulsing like a heart
trapped in a ribcage

I am sorry you were
sawed in half.

REALLY GOOD ADVICE

Patience works
only for so long.

Conflict can be
more effective

and long-lasting.
Harmony sounds good

but don't get
carried away.

In case you were wondering

Not all bombs explode

If they fall in water

Or on deaf ears

Or some other soft landing

Or with a faulty trigger

They just lie there

Like an unfinished conversation

The kind you don't

want to have.

TESTIMONY

A girl, too young
to defend herself
or to know
what was right
and proper
was molested
by a man she knew.

Everyone found out
except her, she was
too young
to remember
and no one
had the courage
to tell her
what happened.

The event became
a center
of silence
around which
her relationships turned
all conversations kept
a distance
from the high
voltage
void.

The adults
never appeared
everyone aged
slowly
discovered neglect
was not everything
only a stipulation
of upbringing.

Who really wants to know
how faceless
and spineless
people supposed to love you
can be.
There are no rules
only assumptions ignored,
pacts rewritten
to suit
the cowardly.

Meanwhile a girl
still suffers
as we all do
and the truth
will not be told.

STRANGE LAND

Painful to leave.
Painful to stay.

Doctors both places
who examine you
give you faint hope.

The ferry sails, the plane lifts off
and you can't touch bottom.
You float like a cork
on the water of your own body.

You check your pockets
take out the memories
disintegrating between your fingers.

The light is stronger
more blinding.
Night comes on faster.

Try to sleep.
Maybe tomorrow
it will not
hurt as much.

SOLIDARITY

for A.H. Я.

I returned to Siberia
the village of my childhood
my aging relatives
wrinkled and sick
in multiple ways
an ambulance for my uncle
the day after Christmas.

My husband and I
went walking—
forty-five below—
avoiding streets
where wolf packs
snap up neighbors' dogs.
The tip of his nose
turned white so
we had to go back.

They said
there would be
no helicopters
the first two weeks
of January
so I bribed a driver
to get us out of there
ten hours in his car
down a frozen river
to the nearest station town.
Luckily when we passed
a car capsized
in the ice

my husband
was asleep.

Three days on the train and
we were in Moscow.
Liberated! I am Russian,
but not solely. My roots
are Ukraine and Romania.
I do not believe
in Mother Russia
who eats her neighbors
and exiles their children.

When we came home
to our apartment
in Athens it was fifteen
celsius. I went to the beach
three days in a row to lie
in the sun. That was two weeks
ago and I have been sick
ever since. I am five feet tall
thin as a rail. I speak seven languages.
I have a daughter and a dog.
My name is Anna.
What's yours?

IF VLADIMIR PUTIN COULD DIE FROM PERIODONTITIS

As his dental hygienist
you would say

he has no pockets
no bone loss

good color and adhesion
ignoring the blood

so you retain
your extra privilege

and perhaps
in the back of your soul

you feel some solidarity
with ex-soviets

the ones Russia keeps trying
to put back in her mouth

to fill the gaps her tongue
incessantly explores.

It is this obsession
he can't stand

though it is all a lost cause
and whatever you say

will fall on welcome ears
as long as it is not the truth.

THE NAZIS ARE IN THE STREETS AND ON THE TROLLEYS

Take your plate
to the sink.

We will see
the news at six.

Keep the curtains
closed.

Only one light on
at a time.

Enough
has happened.

We don't need more
to happen.

Do not answer
that door.

POINT OF USE

The microchips
in my phone
are too heavy

with tanks,
blood, corpses,
rubble, floods.

I can't bear it.
My body strains.
I lean forward,

bash my eyes
on the stack
of images.

My connection
to the world is crafted
by destruction.

WORKING AT THE UN INTERNATIONAL CRIME TRIBUNAL

after The Croatian War

I want justice served
But I cannot translate
With my eyes full of tears.

REMNANT

Statue of Lenin on an armored car pedestal,
Finland Station, St. Petersburg

In this way you will be liberated
from yourself, fall
in service to squares, steel and gunsights.
The unconvinced will be riddled,
removed, and renounced, and I
will stand here in frozen proclamation,
my own ideal, a tiny triumph over
the failure of history to be merciful.

POSSIBLE

It is possible, and perhaps
the definition of grace
that injury (there are so many,
great and small) can be healed,
not denied or ignored,
not covered by silence,
lies, or time; healed and
become a relic that we see
as in a museum of ancient
culture, in disbelief
that this was ever the case,
grateful not to understand.

4

ABSOLUTE UNKNOWING

A great place to start
for avoiding
infinite cycles
of illusion.

But good luck
finding a date
or making it
to old age.

WEIGHT

The meditation instructor said,
"Pick up your rock one more time,"
and I'm thinking,
Again with the rock,
when are we going to do
the twenty minute sitting.
Isn't that
what we're here for?
"Now imagine some difficulty
or challenge in your life—
it could be something small—
and imagine instilling that
into the rock.
And when you're ready
place your rock back down
and let it go."
So I took my impatience
and let the rock have it.
I put it down
and was ready
in a different way.

ADVANCED MATHEMATICS

Do not count on
things adding up.

Even one plus one
can be humiliating.

WHAT CAME FIRST

In the beginning was the chicken
brooding for several eternities
until the last eternity
when she laid an egg
brooded some more
until the shell cracked
and the rooster came out.

The rooster pecked at the stars
and grew bright in tail,
comb and breast, took his mother
and begat a flock as the wheels
of creation spun faster,
the chicken lost all sense of eternity
and replication became
more important than order.

You should be so proud

I don't know
what the congregants
were thinking
when the Rabbi asked
for me to approach
the bima
to read my part
of the torah
and fulfill
my bar-mitzvah duty
and I wasn't there.

I was in
the toilet stall.

I told myself
I couldn't do it
though I had practiced
I could not stand
before the hungry eyes
of the crowd
my grandparents'
friends and acquaintances
to suffer
their judgment.

My father arrived
I told him
to leave.
The my uncle came.
I told him
I wasn't doing it.

He said
I couldn't really
get around it.
If I came out
we could see
how it goes.
Which is when
I started vomiting.

I don't know
what they were thinking
out in the sanctuary
but when my stomach
was emptied
finished convulsing
I opened the door
of my cell
and let myself
be led
to the sacrificial
altar.

Without a glance
at the pews
I walked
up the steps
over to the podium
read the opening prayers
then my haftorah.

Still not looking up
I walked back
down the aisle
to where my family

was seated.
My grandmother said,
Lift up your head, honey.
Now you're a man.

SECRET

Come closer,
listen

to what I never revealed
to what I wove

into the fibers
of my body

I am less than I appear—
me and my ancestors.

Just don't tell
the children.

FATHER'S DAY

In the morning
I stained
the porch stair railing.

Over breakfast opened gifts
with my wife and
talked on the phone.

I felt overrated.
My kids are decent
human beings.

My wife left.
There was no one
to pretend for.

I called up my step-father
and my father.
Was the son.

In the afternoon
I repaired
the toilet.

OVERSEER

I am not afraid
of ruins.

They are simply
another place
to build.

RECUPERATION

My mother got a new hip—
They sawed off the old one,
glued in a new one
and sent her home,
stubborn and weepy on painkillers.

My dad kept track of
her moods and pills.
My wife forced her
to do foot flexes and I
kept the ktichen humming.

We had to be patient,
more than usual,
as my mother
does not
take direction well.

Within a few days
she was pushing the dog
out of her way with her walker
and telling my dad
when, where, and how
to run the sweeper.

It was time to leave.

IMAGINE

a geometric plane
that stretches
in all directions
meets every person
just below the chin

their faces
are all that's visible
sufficient
for the divinity
to show
without the hemming
and hawing
of bodies

imagine a person
really seen
and heard
what they could do
with that

THERE'S ONLY ONE FIRST TIME

We walked up the slope, quarry
walls of corrugated stone rose
in earth tones around us,
long grass matted in paddocks,
pond populated with cattails, frogs,
rock cliffs striated like time,
peaks dotted with bird silhouettes,
and the sky on high, open and wide
as if to lift us from above.

Music

Time is silent.

Space is also silent.

Who are we to enter?

What silence do we have to add

What sound do we have to add

that is worthy

of silence—

Vacationland

The old ocean is of course indifferent,
cycling its tides, as the gray pudgy man
sits on his folding chair at the entrance
to the parking lot, $15 per day,
occasionally waving his neon orange flag
half-heartedly. Does he own the lot? Does he
get paid by the hour or per car? It doesn't matter
much, even to him, the day broken
by conversations, betting on basketball,
the lottery, looking at gals in bikinis,
parents pushing strollers, the line of cars
at the stop sign getting longer, shorter,
an orange Charger with the windows open,
waves of rhythmic music thumping.
It's different every day.

MICHAEL FAVALA GOLDMAN (b.1966) is a poet, jazz clarinetist and translator of Danish literature. Among his sixteen translated books is *Dependency* by Tove Ditlevsen, which made the New York Times Best 10 Books of 2021 as book three of *The Copenhagen Trilogy*. Michael's seven books of original poetry include *Small Sovereign*, which won the 2022 Los Angeles Book Festival in the poetry category. His work has appeared in dozens of publications including *The New Yorker*, *Rattle*, and *The Harvard Review*. He lives in Northampton, MA, where he has been running bi-monthly poetry critique groups since 2018.

https://michaelfavalagoldman.com

www.ingramcontent.com/pod-product-compliance
Lightning Source LLC
Chambersburg PA
CBHW011216120626
46545CB00008B/3024